The Dog

(n) A therapist with fur and four legs.

This edition published by Ravette Publishing 2019.

Ravette Publishing Limited
PO Box 876, Horsham, West Sussex RH12 9GH
info@ravettepub.co.uk
www.ravette.co.uk

ISBN: 978-1-84161-412-0

Dogs

(n) Small rays of light caught on earth for a short time to brighten our days.

URBAN WORDS

RAVETTE PUBLISHING

Sofa

(n) An item of furniture that the dog treats like a napkin.

URBAN
WORDS

Pawesome

(n) What
your
dog thinks
you are.

Drool

(n) What automatically happens when humans sit down to eat or wear anything new.

URBAN
WORDS

Scooby-Don't

(n) Disaster-prone real world version of the animated character.

Puppy

(n) A source of happiness.

URBAN WORDS

Lead

(n) A strap that attaches to your collar which allows you to take your human wherever you want to go.

URBAN WORDS

Deafness

(n) An illness that only occurs in dogs when you need them to come indoors.

URBAN WORDS

Thunder

(n) A signal that the world is coming to an end.

Mud

(n) Wet, dirty substance used for gardening.

See also: Dog Magnet

URBAN WORDS

Pug Life

(n) If you can't eat it or play with it, just pee on it and run away.

Fur-apy

(n) Sometimes cuddling with your dog is the only cure for a bad day.

URBAN WORDS

Muttella

(n) The default name for the filling of any sandwich that the dog has just licked.

Dog

(n) Furry creature who loves you more than he loves himself.

URBAN WORDS

Rover-Dose

(n) When you seem to be acquiring more dogs than you have room for.

Bath

(n) A process owners use to drench the floor, walls and themselves.

PawMa

(n) A woman who proudly claims that her children's dogs are her Granddogs.

Pup

(n) A bundle of pure love gift wrapped in fur.

URBAN
WORDS

Pawkies

(n) What you're telling when you say 'It wasn't me, it was the dog'.

Trans-furmation

(n) What happens when the dog returns from the groomer.

Fartlapse

(n) When the dog gets up and moves a few seconds before you get a whiff of what just happened.

Oppaw-tunity

(n) When your back is turned and the dog steals food from the counter.

Shoe

(n) Favourite dog toy.

URBAN
WORDS

Dog Bed

(n) Any soft, clean, cushioned surface, preferably white.

URBAN WORDS

Goal

(n) To be as good a person in life as my dog thinks I am.

URBAN WORDS

Door

(n) A piece of wood that the dog likes you to open and close repeatedly throughout the day.

Law

(n) Dog rules:
If I like it, it's mine.
If it's in my
mouth, it's mine.
If I can take it from
you, it's mine.
If I had it a little
while ago, it's mine.

Pupside Down

(n) How to describe the state of your home after the destruction caused by a new puppy.

Move

(n) Something you cannot do if the dog is sleeping on you.

Home

(n) Wherever my dog is.